GRANDMOTHER EARTH XIII: 2008

Frances Brinkley Cowden
Editor

Mary Frances Broome
Marcelle Z. Nia
Editorial Assistants

Featuring
Award-winning
Poetry and Prose
from the

2007 GRANDMOTHER EARTH NATIONAL WRITING CONTEST

GRANDMOTHER EARTH CREATIONS
Cordova, Tennessee

Cover Photo: The Ikebana Bridge at Audubon Park by Isabel Joshlin Glaser.

ISBN 1-884289-37-1 10.00

FIRST EDITION: 2008
GRANDMOTHER EARTH CREATIONS
P. O. Box 2018
Cordova, TN 38088
Phone: (901) 309-3692
gmoearth@aol.com
www.grandmotherearth.org

CONTINUING VIEW

Pretending is a delicate wing
layered with ebony feathers.
You are crow in air. You see
below, above, beside yourself
all that is and can be. You

become that sage green ribbon,
weave a fluid fence. Your tapestry
sprouts trees that reach toward yellow,
curve toward shades of life. Lavender
hues, all purple and red. A puddle
of children. Call all
crows. Glossy feathers perch in trees,
speckle the air, draw close
as children stoop to ground.

Begin the lesson of feathers.
These children open eyes.
Their pupils dilate. They continue
their view through veined leaves
up close, transparent and forever real

until they blink. Dark lashes
skim their cheeks silent as a wing.

Carol Carpenter

FARMER'S MARKET

It isn't okra cut small and tender the way
    we know it should be, or
tomatoes whose imperfections declare them
    simon-pure, or
peas bursting from their purple hulls
(their remembered anthem sung on summer-
    morning streets,
"Peas..." with soft refrain, "already shelled)"—
we come for none of these, though we ask the
    price at each tailgate.
We're here to see hardy faces (our parents and
    grandparents with different features)
smile a warranty on produce knowing hands and
    bent backs coaxed to life.
We tender crisp dollar bills, drop quarters
    into calloused palms and
purchase affirmation.
For we need to hear the vernacular of hill,
    prairie and delta in
words carefully weeded from our city talk,
have our nostrils sting from manure on boots,
smell musk of frying bacon lingering in work shirts.
Only here can we feel Dallis grass switch our ankles,
    blackberry briers c1aw our legs,
hear the night call of the whippoorwill,
    see its red eye pierce the dark, and
know that we did not dream childhood.

Marcia Camp

THE FIFTY THINGS WRONG WITH THIS PICTURE

None of this will hasten
or delay that dazzling flash
astonishingly brief on the horizon.
Some of these children have never seen
a river or an orchard or a pea pod
before today. Poppies and impatiens
that make you think "cinnamon"
instead of "cinnabar" perhaps
are in simultaneous bloom
with tiger lilies and chicory
along the road and bachelor buttons
and clematis near the porch.
The children are without dread.
They investigate every crevice
for the golden apples they've heard
about. Only this morning
a man in khaki drove a green tractor through
"that protected section
yonder" beyond which coal is being stripped,
Two starlings chase a sparrow
veering crazily but not dropping
the bread crust from its beak.
Not one detail here depends
on any other, not even the boy
in the chocolate and lemon polo shirt
about to discover a handful of bees.

Timothy Russell

FIREBALL

"They're throwing fireworks at me,"
he frets at his first display, cowers
as if some giant lobs sizzling comets
from beyond the tree line and roller coasters.
Then he rallies as only
a three-year-old can, plants a stance
in parched grass to hurl imaginary rockets
into the face of the intimidating sky.

"I need one," he tells me.
"What color?" "Blue."
I pass the invisible missile,
spinning ball of chi
he grasps in cocksure palm.
Pitch perfectly timed--
an eruption of sparkly zig-zags
quilts the smoke and moonlight.

We both rock back. His astonished eyes
ignite their own blaze, the delight
of unrealized power. After
the apocalyptic finale, our van snaking
through traffic, he still palms fireballs.
"I have two left," he confides.
"I'll throw them when we get home."

What a spectacle he must envision,
sky splattered with explosions
like a pyrotechnic spin painting.
The neighbors will run to gawk,
the big kids gape at his powers,
master of blast-off and flame.

Every dog on the block will bay
at the heavenly bodies he sets into orbit.
With skyward noses, they'll howl his praise.

Nancy Breen

originally appeared in the literary magazine *fresh boiled peanuts*, © 2005

mid-October snow
sunflowers drooping
with the extra weight

Patricia Laster

From: *Haiku Headlines*

still paddles
a canoeist basks
in shimmering lake

Patricia Laster

From: *Season's Greetings Letters 08*

IT WAS MORNING

He died May 9th
holding my hand
twelve hours labored
to leave

4:40 AM
he asked me
with his eyes
how to say goodbye

I said
like the days we paddled
in Waterbury
having driven separate cars.
like at the stop sign
where you always pulled up beside me
when you looked left
through your window
and I looked right through mine
each having different signals
flashing towards home
you would toss me
a kiss
wave one last time
and as you accelerated to turn north
I accelerated to turn south
there was only sadness that a great day
couldn't last forever

I watched in my rear view mirror
your taillights fade into night.

Lené Gary

TO THE GARDEN ALONE

Long years later—too late, really—he was told
he could go back and have a look around the old place,
where tradition would say it had started, from wet clay
to three crosses hammered into a dry, cracked hilltop.

He made the return trip alone:
his Evie was gone by then,
dead of heartache and whatever ills
her affinity for the wrong food had brought on.
So he donned his best suit and his dapper hat,
the one she had always liked. Oh, Isha, Evie,
she would clasp her hands and smile at him
admiringly. The children came like little apes
to stare. The younger boy would laugh aloud
and dance. That boy. He never could keep still,
not his feet nor his mouth either. Well,
he is quiet now. Since that dreadful day
his blood screamed aloud from the very ground,
and the older one stood, dark and sullen
as a shadow, till his mother
and the Landlord cried out, too—
"What have you done?
Where is your brother?"

The old man shakes himself and tries the gate. Good
Lord,
he'd thought the place would still be
cultivated, never dreamed there'd be
such ramblers, brambles, stalky vegetables
and fly-blown fruit, roots polluted with
all manner of grubs and slugs.

And in the center, the dark-branched tree

still bearing fruit. That opulent, glowing
blood red globe which, cut crosswise,
breaks open to a core whose shape
is roughly cruciforn, with seeds like thorn.

Carol Clark Williams

VIETNAM MEMORIAL

They come in clusters,
children too young to know,
students reconciling history, the curious;
but mostly those who held a stake in it:
sweethearts, fathers, siblings, comrades.

Mothers, never able to forget,
lean heavy on the wall searching,
then finger the inscription as if to silence
the sticky nightmares that followed them home,
kiss each letter as if to breathe
life back to the bones
now cooler than the granite guarding their names.

I sit here somber,
brought to a simmering boil,
and I wonder: What does it matter now
that their names are etched in stone.

N. Colwell Snell

FOR MY PARENTS

Spilling like a burst yolk over the earth,
summer fooled me.
I thought I would loll in lush vines forever
but I was greedy for the gold of autumns past.

I flew north to seek in crisper air
the perfect health of every robust cheek
the permanence
of crimson trees that never drop a leaf.

Memories did not give me cause to think
all things return to earth. The pumpkin rots
at the soil line and tough-skinned
gourds crack with winter's weight.

It was your garden's reek that stung my nostrils
and sent my head reeling with
the acrid odor of decay.
I kicked at tarnished leaves, while you
limped silently beside me with your cane.
Mother groped at spotted parsley sprigs
then passed us—tranced.

I planted crocus
(what else was there to do)
and hoped their purple promise
would delay
the barren twig, the brittle gray
the chilling finger of that awful day.

Anna DeMay

POESY

Oh, to write like Ogden Nash!
That would make non-dancers dance.
"May I waltz with you, Ogden dear?"
"I hardly think that's why you're here. You're here
Because you think I will tell you secrets of my trade,
But I won't. It might make you afraid
Of not having a voice of your own,
Borrowing someone else's tone.
My advice to you is not to be carryin'
The desire to become a fun Ogdenarian.
You don't want to dance; you want to sit down with
pen.
(Well, I suppose it would be fine to dance now and
then.)
I'll tell you what: why don't we do both?
Pretty yourself, and I'll get my coat.
But I'll only go if you look very dashing
And we say no more of Ogdening or Nashing."
(It was hard to agree, but I happily did
As onto the dance floor we inkily slid.)

Lois Batchelor Howard

Clematis climbs up
window frame and onto roof
catching spring time rain

LaVonne Schoneman

REMNANTS OF PAST GENERATIONS

(Deserted Homeplace)

An oak tree emblazoned by lightning—
with peeled-back bark exposing parched *limbs.*
A pecan tree hollowed by disease
with choked vines gasping for cooling *breaths.*
A Catalpa tree devoured by worms
with leaves tom apart by hungry *mouths.*
An arbor stripped of its foundation
with decayed grapes bulging from stretched
skins.
A brick chimney wrapped up in brambles—
with crumbled walls gaping at the *joints.*

All surrounding a skeleton frame—
resisting its final collapse.

Jane E. Allen

House at Waggy's Creek, VA, where Jane was born

timid fledgling clings
teetering on edge of nest
mama chirps nearby

Gloria Milbrath

TSUNAMI

A wave came
And took the world
Away

Susanne Leeds

SENRYU

Like wartime soldiers
Raindrops dancing on windshields
March to their demise.

Laurie Boulton

NOBODY LIKES A SNITCH

I visited a friend today
and met her dog, named "Pug."
It seems he is well-mannered and
has his own special rug.

She said. "He always lies down there;
I certainly can vouch
he never jumps on furniture—
no dog hairs on my couch!"

When she went to the kitchen, he
jumped on her easy chair;
but when he heard her coming back
he hopped right off of there.

When she returned, I laughed and said
that Pug had not been "good"
and from the dirty look I got
I know he understood!

Dena R. Gorrell

CLEANER PLUMBING

There's a popular fizzy drink
That can clean your drains in a wink.
It makes my poor brain puzzle and think,
Will my innards react like the sink?

Gloria Milbrath

A HEX ON MY GREEN-THUMBED RIVAL

May your shovel break, may your fertilizer bake,
May your droughts be long and dusty.
May roles make holes, may blights take tolls,
May your pruning tools get rusty.
A killing frost on the hybrids you crossed,
May your prize chrysanthemums sicken.
A pox on your phlox, may your seeds fall on rocks,
May your aphids and mealy-bugs thicken.
To add to your woes, may you slice up your hose
When you run your power mower.
One last incantation: while you're on vacation
May stinkweeds grow up to your door.
Next Garden Show I'll make them know,
You shouldn't win first prize--
My brow with sweat is twice as wet
And twice as green are my eyes!

Glenna Holloway

DROUGHT

My soul drops brown needles
on the parched forest floor,
and I crave the desert
where roots
know how to find
a hidden spring.

Donna Kennedy

MY ZIPPER'S STUCK

My zipper's stuck.
I grimace, frown.
The darn thing won't move up or down.
Our Yankee ingenuity
invented for efficiency
a gizmo on a trolley track
that sometimes won't budge forth or back.

My zipper's stuck.
I grease the slide
with Vaseline. It still won't glide.
I squirm and wiggle, try to shed
my jacket. It won't clear my head,
but tightens at my throat. I choke
and curse the metal rung that broke.

My zipper's stuck,
and I can see
that it will be the death of me,
that like a turtle I must dwell
forever soldered to my shell.
My fate I must emote,
for surely I shall melt away,
succumb on Independence Day
from heat prostration in my winter coat.

My zipper's stuck.

Russell H. Strauss

SILENT WORDS*

They reverently pulled me from the rubble,
dark, cold rains kept pouring down.
My wide gaping holes were torn and jagged,
they tenderly held me limp and ragged;
in sorrow I cried.

They lifted me high for all to see,
my colors soaked in tears of pain,
still grieving, I tried to wave back at them,
but because of revengeful countrymen,
in shame I cried.

They raised me tenderly to wave up there,
high in the wind, though torn to shreds.
For our freedoms I waved proudly unfurled,
sharing all my brutal scars with the world,
humbly I cried.

I've been in battle with many brave men,
and stood for truth in justice halls,
now I stand vigil over peoples' pain
amidst a battle to nobody's gain,
in disbelief I cried.

Soon, I'll wave briskly in this heartland wind
where love abounds, and hate can't win.
My stars and stripes are tattered now, but then
my wounds will heal, and I'll wave whole again,
in honor I cried.

Mary M. Chase

***One day I watched rescuers grappling for survivors in the ruins of the Alfred P. Murrah Federal Building in downtown Oklahoma City. I saw them pull from the rubble a limp, bomb-shredded flag soaked with rain. They raised it for all to see. It dripped, as if weeping from its pain and sorrow. I wept at the sight also.**

Editors Note: our apologies to Mary M. Chase. This poem was printed in Grandmother XIII but was attributed to the wrong poet.

EARLY MEMORY

We heard the wagons coming
loaded with picked cotton soft and white.
Two mules strained to pull it up the hill
and stopped when Dad said "whoa."

I wanted to feel it, jump in it.
Edward climbed onto the wagon, I followed and fell.
My arm was crooked.
Dr. Allen came with his bag.

He mixed the plaster cast with water.
Hot, heavy and itchy for six long weeks.
Mother made tea cakes and read Mother Goose.
Dad looked tired and worried. It was 1932.

Martha McNatt

VOICE OF THE STARS

Africa
I surveyed this ivory continent
as ebony winds
riffled big-game jungle realities
through my mind…
whining mountains...streams...
modern cities…the walled Casbah where
truth stared… stark…naked in the filtered light
and night came creeping
on tenuous feet
stretching across Sahara's
blooded sand
where Rommel met Montgomery hand to hand
across Ethiopia's starving wastelands
into Kenya's safari bush
heavy with bone
and black-skinned natives
silent as stone.

Following mahogany moon tracks
into Casablanca,
I thought of Bergman and Bogart
on those sensuous streets…
knew the haunting enchantment
of African beasts…
knew the lion's breath
hot at the door
and a peace beyond moonlight or Mars…
a strange revelation deeper than death.
I discovered the voice of the stars.

Frieda Beasley Dorris

SUMMER'S BREATH

Hands laced around a mug of steaming
coffee, the tall wiry man settles
onto a weathered stone bench, studies
the pale persimmon moon fading
in the October sky, recalls the night
a jasmine-scented summer wind floated
through the windows of his heart, how he drew
the drapes lest the fragrance disturb
his slumbering fickle foxglove.

He remembers spring storms that swept
the foxglove to distant hills, left
his room barren, how he sought
the jasmine, found it trimmed,
blooming in another's tended garden.

Drifting clouds shroud the ebbing
moon, bring sharp winds that ruffle
his silver hair, scuttle brittle leaves
across the courtyard. He pulls his collar closer,
ponders the seasons of nature. . . of man,
spring's promise to return summer's blossoms
and, perhaps one night, a soft whispering wind
laden with jasmine breath.

Sarah Hull Gurley

shy cypress maidens
rendezvous in shallow creek
reveal spring tan lines

Sarah Hull Gurley

AN OPEN LETTER TO ROBERT BROWNING

"Grow old along with me
the best is yet to be
the last of life for which the first was made. . ."
by: Robert Browning

Such handsome words. But you were 38
while your Elizabeth was 32
and sweet forever love seemed sure to you.
You could not know how years can devastate
man's bones and brawn. Each summer carriage date,
you quoted poetry to help you woo
your fair Elizabeth, a poet who
developed forms which few could imitate.

When death jerked her away, you learned the truth:
the best of life is gone when old age claws
relentlessly. You waken every day
and wonder why man's wisdom and his youth
do not equate. Each pain becomes a cause
to write more words before you pass away.

Verna Lee Hinegardner

PASCAGOULA: TO VIETNAM AND BACK

Outside the fire hydrant lays down it's life
with the sounds of squealing tires
and crunching gravel.
While the boys out on the edge of the front
porch suck on melting popsicles.
I hear the incoming rounds, drop to my knees,
search for the sanctuary of the dark side
of the refrigerator.

There's rice…I can't... won't eat rice.
My weapon is gone. I've lost my strength.
Digging with bleeding, bone bared fingers,
my muddy, blood soaked grave.
No mother, no father, no wife, no children
to know where I sent my ghosts spiraling
into the mists of alien atmosphere
and surrendered to mud and rice.

Summoning, who me? Still summoning.
Beige and gold worn linoleum swimming in my
eyes pounded by high top black Converse
tennis shoes.
It's O.K. Dad. Come on Dad, it's O.K.
Hands lifting, patting, pulling me back from
this lingering canker, putting the demons to bed.

There's water Dad.
Let's go play in the water.

So, we do.

Madalyn McKnight Stanford

POLLYANNA MAKES NO REPLY

He is such an angry man
thrusting his prominent chin
beetling his thick brows
shouting to be heard.

"You," he once said to me
"What do you know of real life
of the tragedies and heartbreak?"

"You," he once said to me
"Always seeing rainbows
finding the sun in a rainstorm.
what do you know of other people's life
of their despair?"

"You," he once said to me
"Who never has a thought
who never sheds a tear
who never has a worry
what right have you to speak?"

Only in the quiet dark of my bedroom
when day is done
do I permit the mask to slip
do I permit the rainbow to fade
do I permit the rain to fall

gently
gently

Madelyn Eastlund

DEATH IS JUST A STONE AWAY

Behind the old homeplace,
cold, cracked stones
mark the graves
of a pioneer family.
Carved-out names and dates,
and sometimes a sweet verse,
are the only legacy
to their identity.
Children scamper over their bones
and then stop for fear
of stirring up
ancient ghosts.
Birds warble a mournful song
in their memory
and scatter wreaths
of tangled green sage.
The buttery sun and icy
blue sky spread their grief
on these enduring
tombs of long ago.
Suddenly, I realize...that death
is just a stone away.

Jane E. Allen

Cemetery at Old Cahaba, AL, by Jane Allen

BIRTH OF A POND

Listen to the sounds of summer
as clouds form
in the afternoon sun.
It's cool
near the pond
that was sculpted by the yellow dozer.
A woodpecker is drumming
nearby; the soft voice of the breeze
weaves in and out of the red oaks.
Splashes and yip yaps
as the Shepherd pups charge
into the water.
No matter that it's only three feet deep
God and nature will fill it
by winter, swelling to fifteen feet.
The levee packed firmly
will be lush and green.
Cattails will grow
and sway in the wind.
Take a closer look
at the water bugs playing tag
on the brown surface.
Dragonflies dive and dodge
like fighter jets.
The whippoorwill calls at dusk
from the wood's edge.
The young willow bows
where the shallow water rests.
Its soft arms motion for all to come near.
Take a drink
and stay awhile.

Two frogs and a turtle
already call it home.

Angela Logsdon

Photo of the pond by Angela Logsdon

AT A LOSS

Deserted by my muse
once again
I sit without ideas.

Did Frost or Shelley suffer
like this?

Angela Logsdon

FAREWELL TO SUMMER

Night is empty of bird song and my cocker
digs a last desultory hole in the lawn,
burrowing in to sleep under a charcoal sky.
Our restless cat yawns, stretching its graceful
body
and gets a mouse-look in its inscrutable eyes.
A thin wind stirs and prowls, warm and ashy.
In the shriveled pasture, even the crickets drowse.
And somewhere from the woodland, we hear
a coyote's sleepy howl.
Fireflies spangle the shadowed meadow, a cow
makes her mournful wail, and nicotiana
sends a floodtide of fragrance from the garden
where the pale moon dwells.
All the feeling of this time of year expressed
in the long, drawn-out note of the white throat,
as though he were trying to put the last drops
of sweetness, the last rays of sun, the last
of all summer's bloom and tassel into his song.
A farewell to the scorched season
which will soon be gone.
Like a hot breath grazing your arms and neck,
summer sighs as she comes to her slow dreaming
end,
while autumn hovers quietly up around the bend.

Anne-Marie Legan

INDIAN PAINTBRUSHES

Flowers grow
          flickers of orange fire
dancing on green fields under Oklahoma skies.
Like weeds they hold to the worst terrain
and spread everywhere.

They beautify discarded Coors cans
and swarm beneath barbed wire
          filling empty pastures
where Choctaw and Chickasaw long ago hunted.

Once as a boy, I worked the roots of a handful
loose from rocky soil across the gravel road
          running in front of my house
and brought them to my mother's flower garden.

With all the care a ten year old could muster,
I replanted the fire
between petunias and four o'clocks.
There, among the tame flowers
          soon they perished.

"They grow wild; that's just how some things
are meant to be," Momma said
as she watered her carefully tended beds
in the summer heat.

But always
          before she'd go back inside,
she'd walk to the edge of our yard
and look
          across the dusty road
at that fiery red-orange blanket

braving the rough-hewn ground
burning in the last light of day.

Ron Wallace

GHOSTLY BEAUTY

Sometimes a ghostly beauty rides the vibrant air,
as flicker of shadows on a tawny lawn,
shiver of, breeze on golden leaves;
or burns on myriad trees in the turning year,
one glowing leaf in late October
tugging on its bough...
slides on flaming leaves as they fall,
as they swirl in a dying dance,
reminding me that all things pass,
that all things flow—
that we hold nothing of hunger or desire
but trembling moments as they come,
or as they seem in memory—
that we too fall away
into the flowing Beauty.

Winifred Hamrick Farrar

From: *Voices International*, Fall, 1991

MULTIFARIOUS WIND

The wind is a giant.
He chases clouds, sends them
scudding across the sky,
seduces trees to sway
sylphlike as a ballet.
Flags become flapping,
snapping whips in his grasp.

The wind is a devil.
He uproots trees, bends
and twists them into pretzels,
crushes dreams, flattens homes
into piles of kindling
and slings raindrop bullets
against windowpanes.

The wind is a kitten.
He lifts kites high then sends
them dipping and diving,
scatters dandelion fluff
to seed far and wide,
wails and moans as a banshee
and rattles bare limbs like dry bones.

The wind is a lover.
He caresses the back of my neck,
whispers secrets in my ear,
massages my scalp
as he ruffles my hair
and kisses my cheek on his way
to everywhere.

Faye Adams

WIND
Oklahoma, 1935

(inspired by *Woman of the High Plains,*
photograph by Dorothea Lange, 1938)

If only it would stop, so I can hear
bird or cricket song, though I doubt
if they be singing in this infernal dust
and heat. Silence. How I long for it.
No sound but blood rushing through
my veins, my breath whispering.

Back in Tennessee, wind is often
a blessing, cooling hills and valleys.
Oh, sometimes, it turns black and
broody, does its damage and moves on.
It does not scorch your face, scour crops
from the earth, whirl them hundreds
of miles from their homeground.

Dust everywhere, in my eyeballs,
the pores of my skin, the baby's
diaper, the stew simmering on
the stove. We breathe dirt, eat dirt,
drink dirt. It clouds the sky at
high noon, dark and smothery.

I go to sleep to the roar of wind,
dream of cyclones and grass fires,
awake to dust sprinkling my body,
my eyes red-rimmed, nose clogged.
The baby wails, his little screech
like a horde of cicadas. I bathe
his parched, feverish skin with
scummy water. He snubs, sucking
frantically at my drying breasts.

He sleeps at last. I go to the well,
nigh lost in the bank of earth,
wait for the bucket to lower. Wind
tears at my hair, my skirt. I raise
my hand to my aching head, hold
my breath to stifle the weeping.

Elizabeth Howard

OLD BLACK AND WHITE PHOTO

(a pantoum in blank verse)

In the photograph where nothing changes
the two are smiling broadly in the yard,
well blessed with jaunty youth and happiness,
and the sadness of the future is unknown.

The two are smiling broadly in the yard,
where a crooked path cuts through our corner lot,
and the sadness of the future is unknown.
One much taller than the other, don't you see?

Where a crooked path cuts through our corner lot,
my bicycle rests against a large tree stump.
One much taller than the other, don't you see?
The short one is my mother, who died young.

My bicycle rests against a large tree stump
in the picture where two people look so pleased.
The short one is my mother, who died young.
That tall boy was my sister's then sweetheart.

In the picture where two people look so pleased,
my small, short mother stands with tall, lean boy.
That tall boy was my sister's then sweetheart
They're laughing at their difference in size.

My small, short mother stands by tall, lean boy.
He went in uniform to World War II.
They're laughing at their difference in size.
which sister captured when she took the shot.

He went in uniform to World War II
well blessed with jaunty youth and happiness
which sister captured when she took the shot—
in the photograph where nothing changes.

Florence Bruce, Memphis, TN

gray stucco instead
of gray bark forms
bent woodpecker beaks

Sandra O. Hancock

Peaches ripening;
Summer is barreling down
Harvest time draws near.

Lucile Roberts Ray

A PERFECT PINK HOUSE

In loving memory of
Patricia Kramer Houghton
my only sister

Clouds float below
like wisps of pink chiffon

Garden ambiance
imagined fragrances
seduce senses

Ahead mesa-topped bank rises
like sculpture

Eyes drawn downward
pink evolves into delicate heather
heather deepens
into God's compelling blue

Blue edges toward infinity
touches pale citron
suffused with fragile light

Pat always wanted
to live in a pink house

Now she does

Bettye K. Cannizzo

IN LIFE

once in a while
roses bloom
red-velvet fragrant
and thorns grow on rambling vines

muggy honeysuckle-breeze touches
my sun-warmed cheeks
under a picture hat

as I sit in the garden

I paint the scene
read a book
or write a poem
sip lemonade icy-cold

birds serenade
when once in a while
I forget
the chemo flows

Faye Williams Jones

heavenly music
black-robed birds across high wire
Sunday morning choir

Louise Hays

LIKE GRASS PUSHING THROUGH

Grass pushing through cracks.
Old building gives way to age;
Soon my memory.

Soon my memory.
life changes like that house of old;
Permanence is gone.

Permanence
I've forgotten who I was;
What I used to love

What I used to love,
What I've stood for all these years.
Simple happiness.

Simple happiness.
Real life makes that seem futile—
like grass pushing through.

Like grass pushing through
foundations I once thought strong;
how misled I've been.

How misled I've been.
To yield to unnoticed cracks
while pretending strength.

While pretending strength,
Who knows what else has slipped by
Like grass pushing through.

Jennifer A. Jenson

HEALING HANDS AND A HEALING HEART

Now patients come and patients go;
You see a lot of action;
But I'm the only one I know
Who was ever rushed to Jackson.

"Rush 'er to Memphis!" I've always heard.
"It's a case for Dr. Big Name!"
"They rushed 'im to Memphis," we get the word,
"To a doctor of this great fame!"

Big names, big bucks, big stethoscopes
Were all to no avail.
This ailment had them on the ropes!
All Memphis treatments failed!

"Let's rush 'er to Jackson!" the word came down,
"There's a mighty healer there!
There's a Dr. Winston in that town.
Let's put her in his care."

I heard he made a deaf man hear
And made a blind man see!
He heals a thousand folks a year;
That's good enough for me.

I heard a Cadillac gave a moan
As Winston happened by.
He gave it a shot of prednisone.
Now, that sounds like a lie.

But then that Cadillac spun its wheels
And took off like a star!
I'll tell you Dr. Winston heals!
He even healed a car!

Now I've traveled near; I've traveled far;
I've traveled 'round the globe;
And any doc who heals a car,
I believe he could heal Job!

Well, it must have worked, 'cause here I sit
Just making up this rhyme.
I laughed so hard my rib bone split!
IT'S DR. WINSTON TIME!

Rose Camille Parrish

CONTEMPLATE TIME

Red Rock Canyon shows us how passionate life
can be
Crimson skies awake in us an unruffled mind
With neither greed nor anger
Nature beckons us to live with love
Depart like an afternoon gale

Serene maroon terra-cotta mountains
Dance across a desert floor

A chalk white moon sails east.

Vincent J. Tomeo

PHONE CALL FROM MISS MUFFET TO BO PEEP AFTER ARRIVING IN MEMPHIS

Russell H. Strauss

"Bo dear, this is Missy calling you from Tennessee. I arrived Monday by Northwest Airlines. Mother Goose, of course, suggested that I fly by gander, but I prefer the comfort of a jetliner. I experienced an ID problem in the airport when they mistook me for a puppet. Miss Muppet indeed! The flight itself, however, was uneventful.

I wish I could say that I am delighted with Memphis, but the restaurants here are not very exciting. Do you remember the time we dined with the king and all those birds flew out of the pie? Nothing like that here! The nightlife is about as thrilling as when Jack jumped over the candlestick. Neither experience was very entertaining. At least, I have not encountered a spider since I have been here. My exterminator swears he has sprayed for them, but I don't trust him. How often have I found one of those crawly little creatures sitting beside me?

As soon as I arrived, I went shopping for a tuffet. My trademark, you know! Would you believe I must have visited every home furnishing and houseware store in town and not a one of them had a tuffet? I had to settle for an ottoman. My name does not rhyme with ottoman! Then I went to the grocery store and asked for curds and whey. I ended up with cottage cheese and (You will never believe this!) grits. This is some kind of glutinous white stuff they eat for breakfast here. Heaven knows what they make it from!

What will they say of me now? Can you imagine generations of children singing,

'On the ottoman, Miss Muffet sits,
chowing down her cheese and grits'?

When I write, I will enclose some American dollars for Mother Hubbard. Tell her to go grocery shopping. I know she's on a fixed income. I hate to see one of our senior citizens with a bare cupboard. Also, I hear that London Bridge is falling down. I should send a contribution to the repair fund. Before I left home, the preservation people sent me a plea for assistance. The note was very polite, addressing me throughout as, 'My fair lady.'

What's this, dear? You've lost your sheep again? Do you suspect poachers? If not, they'll come home if you leave them alone. I've always said so. Do I think they'll be wagging their tails behind them? Of course, dearie! Have you ever seen sheep with tails in front? Well, dear, (or should I say 'honey lamb?') go look for them if you must! We British girls can't do without our mutton, can we? Bye-bye."

Mockingbirds flee charred
oak corpses unable to
imitate silence.

Russell H. Strauss

HOPE ANN'S CHRISTMAS

Elsie Schmied Knoke

Hope Ann's driveway was still empty when my family and I left for the Christmas Eve service. I thought that was strange, since she was expecting all her family for Christmas; I had even helped her get ready. We bought her tree and helped her decorate it and later, took her around to distribute her fabulous Christmas cookies. She was ready. After we deposited our kids with their Sunday School teachers, my husband, Don, and I found seats near the back of the church. There was Hope Ann, all alone in her new red coat and matching beret. She smiled wanly at us.

When we first moved into the neighborhood ten years ago, Hope Ann came over from next door that afternoon, a chicken casserole in one hand, a plate of warm cookies in the other and a big smile on her plump face. She was a foot shorter than I but a bundle of energy. We learned later that she had been widowed for years and raised their four children alone in the big house she and her husband had built. We knew she was eagerly awaiting the visit of the entire family for Christmas, but apparently they were late.

On Christmas morning, we'd finished unwrapping the packages from Santa and from each other. I wore the emerald green velvet robe I'd wanted and Don seemed to enjoy his Nordic sweater, when the doorbell rang. It was Hope Ann, out of breath and slightly anxious looking.

"Merry Christmas, Hope Ann. Don't you look nice in your new coat."

"Thanks. I can't stay but a minute. Would you keep my house key for awhile? The kids must have been delayed again and I don't want to miss church waiting for them. I'm singing in the choir you know. I left a note on the back door where they can't miss it. I appreciate it." And she dashed off.

About three o'clock that afternoon we were listening to the stereo when I heard a rap on the door. Hope Ann was obviously out of sorts, quite unlike her usual self. "I need another favor." We settled her in the big lounge chair by the fireplace with a cup of cider so she could catch her breath, wondering what had happened.

"I'm simply furious. It's those kids of mine. Not one of them is coming after all. I'm so angry, I've made up my mind to leave my house to the church when I die. Then they won't have to bother with it. I want you to draw me a new will tomorrow. And don't try to talk me out of it."

I looked at Don. "It's her life," he said. "But Hope Ann, please sleep on it."

"But first, I've another favor, if you don't mind. When I got off the phone with my daughter, Sally, I was really annoyed. But I'm not going to let anything spoil my Christmas. So I called Sue, the social worker at the shelter, and she says we can come over there right now." She smiled sweetly and turned to Don. "We'll need your van and Amanda's pickup."

We agreed and bundled up. I told the kids to behave while we were gone, knowing they would probably turn on the TV the minute our backs were turned. Hope Ann rode with me in my pickup and Don followed in the van.

Sue was waiting in her station wagon when we pulled up.

"Hope Ann, I hope you know what you're doing. These people have had so many disappointments in their lives, I won't have them hurt again."

It was obvious that the volunteers who staffed the shelter had tried to make it a little more festive, with red and green crepe paper streamers and an artificial Christmas tree twinkling in one corner. People were sitting on cots and avoiding our eyes. They all had that hopeless look in their eyes. There were at least six or seven of them, old and young, but the most pitiful were the children. I never saw such quiet children, just sitting on the floor nearby, never straying far from their mothers.

"Did you ask them if they were interested, Sue?"

"I'm sure that every one of them would love to come to your home for Christmas dinner."

Hope Ann approached a thin woman with pale blonde hair gathered into a pony tail and tied with a shoe lace. She held a baby that looked to be about three months old. A runny-nosed boy of about two clung to his mother's slacks.

"Would you like to come to my house for dinner today? It's nice and warm and I've got the biggest Christmas tree. A real one," she said to the boy. He hid his face in his mother's lap.

"It would be nice to be in a real house for Christmas," the woman agreed, "even just for dinner. It's been a long time since we lost our home."

Hope Ann walked over to another young mother with a set of school-age twins, a boy and girl, who seemed thrilled at the prospect. Then she spotted an old woman in the corner, a bag full of belongings clutched in her arms, peering suspiciously at us.

"What do you want? A bunch of do-gooders, I suppose."

Hope Ann shooed us away and talked quietly with the woman. About ten minutes later, the two joined us. "Might as well," said the woman. "Got nothing better to do. Kids all too busy to even know I was evicted."

Sue brought two pale young men and a pair of sisters who appeared to be seventy or so. They chirped like birds, looking forward to a family holiday time, their words falling all over each other in their eagerness to tell us all about the old days. The men seemed to be too tired to talk.

"I have room for one more," said Hope Ann. "How about that tall fellow over there? He looks like he lost his last friend. We can't leave him here alone."

We piled everyone into our van and Sue's station wagon. The bag lady rode with Hope Ann and me in the pickup. Everyone's belongings went into the truck.

Hope Ann's new friends overcame their misgivings as she hurried them into the house and enlisted their help to put extra leaves in the dining room table. When we opened the door to the living room, the children were transfixed by the giant tree and the wrapped packages beneath. "Can I put the lights on?" asked one of the twins.

"Of course," said Hope Ann. "Now some of you come into the kitchen and help me bring the food out. It's keeping warm in the oven."

The following day Hope Ann came over to redo her will. I have my law office in the front of the house so I can be home for the family. Most of my work deals with contracts, wills and deeds with only an occasional court case.

"This was the best Christmas ever, just the tonic I needed. You should have seen them open the presents I had for my grandchildren. They were thrilled to death." She sighed happily. "One mother kept saying they had nowhere to keep those things, especially after I gave them the presents I bought for my kids. Granted, some things don't fit, but we can exchange them."

"Sounds like you plan to keep in touch."

"Absolutely. In fact, I invited them to stay with me." She smiled again. "Wait until my kids hear that. But it's my house and if they won't even come to visit, people who need it might as well use it, right?"

I was stunned by her generosity. "You're not serious. All twelve?"

"Why not? I've plenty of room. The men set up beds I had stored away in the attic and cleaned up the crib. Good thing I never threw them away. Clifford always accused me of being a pack rat, but now we're going to have a wonderful time, just wait and see."

And you know, they are. The two mothers share a job answering phones in a small office. Each works two days while the other cares for the children. Agnes, the bag lady, turned out to be a retired short-order cook who is too frail to work more than an hour or two at a time; she cooks and the others help her. Matthew, the withdrawn man who seemed so confused, had been unceremoniously evicted when he couldn't pay the rent. When I checked into the matter, it seems that someone had stolen his Social Security checks. So he and I arranged for his future payments to be deposited directly into a bank account that we set up for him.

He said, "My wife handled the money in our house and didn't believe in banks. But when she died, I kind of let things slide, didn't care. Hope Ann is a godsend. I can pay my way, too."

"I'm sure she will appreciate that. Perhaps you can fix things around the house. There's always something going wrong in this old house."

He beamed. "Do you think you could do something for those poor young fellows? They don't talk much and neither one eats enough to fill a bird. Seems like something's wrong with the dark-haired one."

The very next day, Thomas, the dark-haired one, collapsed on the kitchen floor when he was setting the table. When his friend, Charles, returned, from the store, I was in the kitchen with Hope Ann.

"I guess you'll want us to move now. You've been so kind and we really appreciate it, so we'll understand if you do."

"Now, Charles, sit down here and have some tea. What's wrong with Thomas? Why should we want you to move?"

I had a feeling I knew what the problem was and hesitated to hear it, but Hope Ann motioned me to remain.

"You must have noticed that Thomas doesn't look well," he started. "He's HIV positive and now he's got pneumonia. They want to keep him in the hospital until he gets better." He sank his head into his hands.

"He'll be fine, don't you worry," said Hope Ann, patting his shoulder. "The best thing to do for him is to take care of yourself. And don't even think about moving out. I knew he was sick. This house has seen plenty of sickness in its day." She smiled reassuringly at him. "My grandmother had typhoid, and two of my brothers died in the flu epidemic right after the First World War."

Charles smiled wanly. "Our families refused to let us come home once they knew we were . . . you know, . . . gay. I had to quit working when Thomas got sick. Then our apartment was broken into and we were beaten and robbed. The landlord used that as an excuse to kick us out. Then Thomas got worse."

"Well, have something to eat and we'll talk about it later."

Now Charles works sporadically as a free-lance writer while Matthew fixes things. Right now he's working on Hope Ann's old car. He thinks he might get it running again, being a shade tree mechanic. With the help of Hope Ann, the two old sisters and the young mothers, Agnes keeps them all well fed. Everyone pitches in with money as they can afford it. And the two sisters finally got the insurance money from the fire that burned their house down and have decided to stay with Hope Ann and the others.

Last Christmas, Hope Ann, my next door neighbor made her own happiness. Today she has a noisy house full of people, eating her food and keeping her company; she's loving every minute of it. And when Hope Ann's family decides to pay her a visit, they stay in a motel and eat in restaurants.

A TOMCAT NAMED AUNT BEA

Jerré Carter

First off, let's get this straight. I ain't no girl, see. Just because those humans don't know better and allowed this little person to name me don't mean I'm no broad. I'm a guy. Up until now I thought of myself as Gus. Now I'm referred to as Aunt Bea. Aunt Bea, for gosh sake, what kind of a name is that for a self-respecting cat? There's no figuring out these humans.

As for me, I was getting along okay, bumming around like always, some times leaner than others, but I'm out on the open road, no strings, no cares, and the smell of honeysuckle in the air. I had just seen some juicy birds eating out of a feeder on a deck right by a house. The feeder is set just low enough for me to make a leap into it. I got' em in my sights and bam, I jump onto the ledge, but instead of getting a mouthful of luscious foul, I end up with a chop full of seeds.

Now this wasn't embarrassing enough, but out comes this grandma-type lady. Here I am, caught in the act, trying to figure out what to do, when all of a sudden I hear this person saying, "Oh, you poor thing. You are so skinny and now you're reduced to eating birdseed. Poor baby, wait just a minute and I'll get you some nice milk."

I'm stunned. I'm still up to my paws in birdseed, unable to move because I'm so confused, when out she comes again, bearing a big bowl of milk and urging me to drink. I don't want her to think I'm easy, so I jump off and start to slink away. Sure enough, she calls me back, begging me to drink.

Well, I hate to snub her hospitality, so I go over and start sniffing. Hmm, I can still remember how good it smelled, fresh, cold like it hadn't been in the dumpster any time. I slurp it up, so as not to offend her, you understand. She stands there and beams. She tries to pet me, but I won't have anybody taking liberties with me, so I scram.

A couple of days later I'm in the neighborhood catching grasshoppers for lunch when she sees me. Quick as a wink she comes out with a bowl and sets it down on her deck. Sure enough, when I decide to investigate, it's full of milk. I oblige her by cleaning it up. I come to find out that if I show up, she'll put out. So I start coming to the door looking for her on days when the hunting's not too hot.

One afternoon there was a big human in the house with her. He was rudely telling me to scat. She was telling him the "starving-cat-eating-bird-seed" story and he was laughing his head off and saying it was more likely I was eating birds. What rubbish. I never ate none of them birds in the feeder. Scouts honor. I never could catch a one of 'em. So I soon figure that this guy's not too keen on me being around, see. So I think to myself, I'll show him who's boss. I start coming back every day and the chow gets better. Then I decide, why walk back to find a place to spend the night? I'll just bed down here, close to the old feed bag.

Well, this goes on for a long time; she's happy, I'm happy, he ain't happy, which really makes me happy. One day a taxicab brings her daughter and a two-year-old grandkid to visit. The grandkid appreciates my good looks, which shows he ain't no dummy. The daughter asks my name and the lady says I don't have one and would the grandkid like to name me? Well, it takes this tike about two seconds to destroy my previously high opinion of him.

"Aunt Bea", he shrieks, and everybody says, "Okay, then, that's her name." Her name, what do you mean her name? I'm a guy, see. A tough guy at that. I'm no sissy girl. Good grief What kind of pride could I have with a moniker like that tied around my neck? My name's Gus, for gosh sake, GUS, got it? Seems they didn't and from that day on I was known as Aunt Bea. I never forgot to show my disdain when it was mentioned, but nobody seemed to notice, so after a while I just shrugged my shoulders and ate.

Things went along fine all autumn. I learned that if I went around to the little deck by their bed-room door and snuggled down, she could see me. It wasn't long till out came a box with blankets in it and I was snug as a bug in a rug, right outside his bedroom. He hated that. Especially when I was nice enough to wake them up in the morning by climbing on the sliding screen door. Oh, it's a glorious feeling to start your day off by seeing a man get mad and throw something at his own door.

One night it rained and soaked my bed. The lady petted me and she dried out my bedding. Later that day she came home with a contraption for me to sleep in. It was a new garbage can that she lined with my blankets. Very nice. And by bumping it around just right, I could look straight into the bedroom and give the old guy a stare that would enrage him.

A couple of months later it became very cold and icy. I had to snuggle to the end of my garbage can to get warm. True, I had never been so cozy in winter before, but I thought, maybe I can do better. So as it became colder, I became more visible. The best one yet was to stand outside on the deck, peering into the house with sad, pitiful eyes and raise one limp paw up, like it had a splinter in it, pleading for comfort. It didn't take long. I heard him saying, "No, no, no way," quite often that week as the lady worried about my welfare.

Then low and behold, one morning he went to the garage, mumbling, snarling, talking to himself and started to saw. In no time at all he had made the cutest little cat door I've ever seen. She came and put my box and my food inside by the little door and I was all set for the winter. Not only is it toasty and warm inside the garage, but there are all kinds of places to explore; like his workbench, his boxes, the top of his car. The only time I have to be careful is when he comes down to get in his car. I have to be on my toes and come close enough, but not quite close enough for him to kick me. I let him miss me. That makes him mad. I love it. It's wonderful. She's happy, I'm happy and he's miserable!

THE MASHER

Malu Graham

"Listen, you two, you have to help me out of this mess I am in!"

Jake and I couldn't believe our ears. His sister Madge's conversation usually consists of detailed monologues about her life, in which she—inevitably–is the heroine. "If I hadn't helped Mary face the facts, she'd have made such a mistake..." she'll say. And, "If John didn't have me for a friend, he never..." Or: "--so I sent him the money. I'm too generous--it's just my way." You can imagine what a thrill she is to listen to.

We are in our late sixties now. It isn't as though we're unaccustomed to her long-winded anecdotes. Marriages saved, dogs rescued, friends reconciled—I keep expecting to hear that the President himself has begged for her advice. Jake, my husband, puts up with it by simply not listening. That leaves me to punctuate her run-on sagas with 'uh-huhs,' and 'my, mys.' If I stay silent too long, Madge stops, asks did I 'get that' and repeats from the beginning. It's better to chant accompaniment to her stories.

This time it was different. Here she was on our doorstep, in trouble herself! She only visits twice a year, and usually doesn't stay more than a few days longer than she has originally announced. Madge does have a good heart, mind you, and is sometimes as helpful as she herself thinks she is. Now she was asking our help. Did we dare to hesitate?

What I was hoping was that, this time, *I* would be the heroine.

Her problem was as surprising to us as if she announced that she'd won the Miss America contest. Imagine this scenario: there was this eighty-year-old man she had met (and unselfishly helped, of course) who had fallen passionately (her word) in love with her, and who was driving her crazy with his unwanted attentions. Turning him in to the police would doubtless discourage him, but such a drastic action would add up to total failure, spoiling her long list of successes in helpfulness.

She had decided to visit us earlier than usual this summer to escape his constant phone calls and visits. Fine with us.

I don't like being judgmental, but I have to tell you that Madge is not love's young dream. Even at twenty she didn't turn heads. Her eyes are a bit close together and her mouth rather wide for a narrow face...well, suffice it to say: after the death of her long-suffering husband five years ago, no new man had come knocking on her door. She was a busy widow, nevertheless--busy minding other people's business, and 'helping' them as best she could. Relatives were usually her targets, but in this present dilemma, she had reached out beyond the family circle. (Nieces, nephews, grandchildren must have had a welcome breathing spell.)

At the end of her confession, Jake just looked at her and cleared his throat noisily, a ploy I recognized as a way of stifling laughter. I was trying to keep a straight face myself, knowing that Madge was nothing if not sincere. Mocking her would have been cruel.

"Can't you just tell him you are not interested in a romantic relationship?" I queried. Madge shook her head emphatically.

"I've done that. He won't take no for an answer; keeps saying he just wants to live with me. He is at my door every day, asking and asking."

"What did you do for him that was so endearing?" I couldn't help asking, in spite of my dread of the customary heroic tale.

"Not all that much. I taught him how to play canasta at the Senior center. He's old. It was a diversion for him, playing with the other folks." She went on in her inimitable fashion to describe her work at the senior center, naming and describing several people who were indebted to her for much more than canasta playing. We waited it out. Finally she came to the point. "...but one day, Earl—Mr. Tuttle–offered to drive me home, it was raining --the bus was late; I was worn out."

Jake and I exchanged glances. Drive her home? Mistake number one.

"Now I can't escape him. Turned out he lives about a block away. That very day he started telling me he wanted to live with me."

This seemed odd to us, but we realized that the elderly feel the pressure of Father Time more than younger people and when courting, are inclined to sidestep preliminaries. This codger obviously didn't want to waste time achieving his last dream of happiness. We figured he must be a good listener.

Jake grinned. "So you are being chased by a masher." I looked at him in amazement. My eyebrows rose an inch.

"Masher! That's a word from the roaring twenties! More like a stalker, I'd say." Madge was not interested in terminology.

"***I*** call him a nuisance," she muttered. "And I am not going back home till I can figure out a way to keep him away."

Jake looked at me; I looked at Jake. No words were spoken, but we were communicating like mad. That night we talked in bed for several sleepless hours. By one a.m. we had hatched a plan.

We hit Madge with it the next morning at breakfast. She agreed to it at first with some skepticism, but after several days, could come up with nothing better. In a couple of weeks, we would drive

Madge back to Melody, Mississippi, bivouacking that night at her house. Madge called long distance to her next-door neighbor in Mississippi, and was assured that a gentleman had been coming by daily, hoping to find Madge at home.

We planned to meet the masher at the door. And the day after we arrived in Melody, we did.

He was even more shriveled than we had imagined. It was hard to believe he had the strength to pursue his heart's desire so energetically.

"Is Miz Hanson at home?" he quavered.

Jake pretended to look confused. "Missus who?" he asked. I was standing slightly behind him. Madge was in the kitchen, doubtless rehearsing a future heroic anecdote to herself.

"Miz Hanson. The lady who owns this house." At this Jake smiled kindly and cracked the door a little wider.

"Missus Hanson? Of course--the former owner. Sorry, I can't give you any information about the lady. We closed on this house over a week ago. Just moved in." We will carry that lie to our graves. The look on the old fellow's face was heart rending.

"—But…but I kept asking her! I wanted to live in this house: it is the one I grew up in. I'd have bought it when we moved back down here, but I only just discovered who owned it. I—I—DURN that woman! She never let me explain why I wanted to live in it. That was the talking-est female I ever met. She never even told me she wanted to sell. DURN!"

Jake just stood there, taking it in. After a moment he said "Well, sir, I am sorry to disappoint you…but…"

Mr.Tuttle shrugged and turned away. "I guess there ain't no chance now. I'll have to tell my wife we can make an offer on that house across town that she wanted. We're tired of staying with relatives." He walked slowly to an old Buick parked on the street. We watched him go, feeling like a couple of criminals.

When we tried to explain to Madge, all she heard was the part about his buying a house across town.

"I am glad we thought of telling him the house was sold," she said. She shook her head sadly. "The nerve of that bounder, after all I did for him! Flirting with me—and him a married man!"

EVENTS OF THE DAY

Lois Requist

Feeling fine after working out and showering at the gym, Robert Deal, dressed in beige slacks and a deep blue silk shirt stopped in at Starbucks in Lafayette to get a cafe latte'. Papers would be signed on one property this morning. He spoke briefly to a woman in the café, then smiled and whistled softly as he left. This was going to be a great day!

So much for premonitions.

Latte in hand, he felt a chest pain and crumpled to the sidewalk, the tan liquid sloshing over his pants and onto the concrete. He was gone too soon to hear the wail of the siren, or watch everyone pour out of the coffee shop and gather round him as the paramedics tried in vain to restore his breathing. It was a shame that he was not in a position to enjoy being the center of attention as he was lifted onto a stretcher and put inside the ambulance.

The woman to whom he had spoken as he was leaving saw him fall, called 911, went outside, leaned over him, pushed back his shirt and told the crowd to stay back. Once the ambulance arrived, she retreated, nervously following the medical team's procedures, noting that there was no response from Robert Deal. It seemed pretty certain from looking at the perfectly still body that it was too late for aid or comfort.

Another observer, a regular at Starbucks, Charles Boodingle watched the woman more than the victim. He knew them both by sight, but his instinct for drama told him that what the woman was feeling was *now* the vital part of the story. When the paramedics got ready to leave, she went to her car and followed.

Charles Boodingle brought his substantial girth and presence to Starbucks frequently, watching people coming in or passing by the shop. A collector of human anecdotes, he was a gossip, plain and simple. He jotted a few notes occasionally, had a way with words, and was "going to be a writer" someday, though he lacked discipline. The write-every-day, keep-on-keeping-on required to actually *be* a writer—that was not for Charles. He found it easier and more to his liking to be a local character.

He stepped into Starbucks at approximately 7:35 every morning, wearing a fine quality but worn sports coat, with a leather patch on each elbow, and a demeanor of one content and pleased with the world in spite of being fully aware of its cruelties and ambiguities. He smelled the roses but was aware of the thorns.

A pipe bulged in one jacket pocket. In the summer, he would light it at one of the outside tables, though in Northern California even outside smoking brought frowns from some of the PC types. (They would have to pass another law-he could see them making a mental note). Inside in winter, as was now the case, he occasionally sucked on the unlighted stem.

Each morning and again in mid-afternoon, he held court, talking with whoever decided to come by his table. On the rare occasion that he did not appear, customers coming in at 7:45 looked around, checked their watches, and asked other customers or the servers where Charles was. Walking away, they sensed a vague uneasiness.

Charles stayed away for exactly that purpose, mystery being essential to being a notable local. Those who occasionally sat down next to Charles—he never went to them—shared the friendly "in the know" atmosphere he conveyed and left with the feeling that you never quite knew Charley, as some called him behind his back. Respectful of everyone, he inspired confidence, while saying less than he knew.

Later that day, when Boodingle stopped into Starbucks again to see if any excitement was still rippling from this morning's death, the rhythm of the shop had slowed to its routine pace. Customers who had talked about what they saw and what they knew of the victim had left, or turned back to their newspapers. Sections of the *Contra Costa Times* and the *San Francisco Chronicle* lay around the shop. Sports. Business. News. Entertainment. The ubiquitous sales pages.

Boodingle noticed that the woman who was the last person to speak to Robert Deal had returned to the cafe as well. Her head was buried behind a newspaper.

"Might as well take Robert Deal's card out of the box," said Jason, a pony-tailed clerk at Starbucks, reaching in for the 3 x 5 card, and glancing down at it. "The next cup would have been free."

"Geez, man, that's cold," Doug said over the hiss of the espresso machine. "Don't! Don't do that! Don't tear it up!"

Jason held onto the card and looked at his co-worker. "You know he's not going to be in for coffee again."

"Give it to me," Doug barked, grabbing the card.

"Yeah, man, did you serve the guy?" a woman in jogging clothes said.

"Goes to show, you never know. What did he have?" another customer asked.

"Put the card in the window for a few days. 'In Memoriam.' Out of respect," yet another suggested.

"Boy, that'll bring the customers in droves," Jason said. "He bought a latte. He died."

"I don't think he even tasted it," Doug murmured

"Wow, you mean just holding it brought him down! I'm outta' here, man," a young man whose body was pierced dozens of times said, turning and leaving.

"Just because two unrelated things happen in close proximity, does not prove cause and effect," an older, bearded man said. "Still, I'll have tea."

"Here today, gone today," Jason muttered.

Doug set the card down, glanced over toward his mother, the woman who had last spoken to Deal, and continued working. He didn't know why the two had talked. When she returned to the cafe, she looked drawn and tired.

"Doug," she said with unusual huskiness in her voice, "our plans for tonight have been..." she paused looking around the cafe as if the right word might be hanging in the air or on a table, "cancelled."

"Oh, really, that's too bad. Another time?"

Again, she looked at him with such anguish that he wanted to come around the counter and hug her.

"No." She turned around and sat down.

Doug's sharp disappointment showed momentarily on his face, but a young woman with a child was waiting to give her order. He turned back to his work.

A drop of coffee fell on the card. He picked it up again, wiped away the dark liquid stain, and looked around for a safe place to put it among the rows of paper cups and glass mugs, a pile of plates, pastries waiting to be taken, and tongs for lifting the Danish and croissants. Seeing no other available spot, he set the card atop the computer cash register.

"Just leave it there," he said.

Charles Boodingle, from a table not far away, observed the woman. Probably in her mid-forties, she wore horn-rimmed glasses, a tawny business suit, and had thick brown hair that came to just above her shoulders. The Business Section of the *Chronicle* was in front of her face and the pages quivered slightly in her grasp. She seemed to be reading at the same place for some time.

When Charles noticed Robert Deal speak with the woman earlier that day, it occurred to him that, in the mystery department, she perhaps outdid him. She came into Starbucks infrequently, with no pattern that he could see, spoke to no one that he observed, except the employees, and that briefly, though she sometimes lingered a bit when speaking with Doug.

Finally, Boodingle's curiosity overwhelmed him. He abandoned his general habit, rose, took the few steps to where she sat, and said, "Excuse me, ma'am, I am sorry to intrude. I could not help but notice that the man who died spoke with you just before he left the cafe. May I offer my condolences if he was a relative, or a friend?"

The woman looked up at him. Her eyes from behind dark glasses appeared luminous and wary. She stared up at him for some time, finally saying, "Thank you. It's all right."

"You did not know him well, then?" Charles asked.

"No, though a long time ago he was my friend...my lover."

"No!" Charles was unsure how to proceed, "It has been some time? Other people and things must have taken your—and I suppose his—attention?"

She lowered the paper, hesitated, then gestured for him to sit down. "Yes. It was over twenty years ago. I moved away. I hadn't seen Robert Deal for many years until just a few days ago."

He sat down across from her and waited, knowing that silence often causes people to speak.

"Tonight, I was to introduce him to our son. They never met." As she said this her hands shook and she glanced back over her shoulder to where the cappuccino machine still hissed. She saw Doug pick up the punched card and study it for a minute. Needing to get back to work and still unwilling to throw it away, he lifted his apron and stuffed the card into his front pants pocket. She continued staring at the young man as tears rolled down her cheeks.

Charles watched the woman, following her gaze as it fell on Doug behind the counter. The young man must have sensed her stare, for he halted his coffee preparations and walked around the counter to where she sat. Doug looked at her questioningly, an idea circling at the back of his mind.

Charles stood up abruptly, brushing his hand against the young man's shoulder—"Excuse me," he said and stepped back, though continuing to watch the pair.

"Was he... ?" Doug spoke to his mother.

The woman nodded slightly.

Doug looked a long time at his mother, seeing what now would never be. She was enough. She always had been. Lifting his apron, he pulled out the card, and handed it to her. "I thought you...we...might like to have this, Mother."

Across the room, Charles Boodingle sucked at his unlit pipe and stared out the window, satisfied with the events of the day.

Photograph by Laurie Boulton

2OO7 YOUTH CREATIVITY AWARDS

DANIEL O'NEIL

His last chord was in C minor.
The awkward apex of jumbling C, E flat, and G,
Trickling down guitar strings,
A chilling melodious waterfall
Constricting the coffee shop audience,
With a mocha autumn frost,
Into static ice crystals.
It wasn't a slip of his fingers
Or a malfunctioning microphone.
Simply an eerie cacophony
Of foreboding mood,
Storm clouds on the Monday horizon,
Written by the artist formerly known as O'Neil.
A stale note stinging over musician's graves,
Up people's spines into forlorn silence,
The Westminster chimes of a grandfather clock
In the abandoned hours of the late night.
However, this clock's a time bomb
That questioned the ability of defying fate in vain,
For suffering for his art
Is not the same as a bullet to the brain.
His last chord was in C minor.

A. J. Tirrell

Daniel O'Neil was a victim of the Virginia Tech tragedy

CATCHING BUTTERFLIES

Children smiling on the playground
Swinging high
Touching stars
Holding hands going caterpillar
Maybe next they'll reach for mars

Innocence is a beautiful thing
Not something to waste
Or something to free
Naive can be good sometimes
Especially when they aren't old enough to see

And they don't know it yet
But when they get older
They don't lose the thrill
In catching butterflies

But blindness doesn't last an eternity
They grow up fast
And see one another
They were once friends forever
But now they're lovers

They had known a while it was meant to be
But they were children
And that never dies
They didn't know what young love was
They didn't know about butterflies

And now they know it
And now that they're older
They still feel the thrill
In catching butterflies

Adults sit on the playground
Watching swings
And flying doves
And remember when they were younger
When they didn't know about the feeling of love
Or butterflies

Courtney Watts

Eye-Poem by Luke Cottam

Eye-Poem by Ryan Johnson

In the freezing night
A snowman roams through the cold
As the last leaf falls.

Lucy Hoard

THE TRAIN STOPS

Life is like a
train
It has a start
It has a destination
It starts slow
as when before you
can walk
It goes faster like when you
start to crawl
It leaves the station like when
you don't
sleep in a crib any longer
It gets more speed as
when you learn to ride a bike
It gains more speed as when
you learn to drive
all the twists and turns are
like your bad times
the straight your good
I see the other train station
as a nursing home
close to the end but not quite
The slow down is you
slowly dying
you know it will happen
But it has not yet
as you slow down more
you are closer and closer to death
you have already
retired
as you
come towards a gentle slow stop

you are on an
oxygen tank
to you it is obvious
to everyone else there is
hope
then it comes
you die, the train stops
and the new life begins.

James Apple

MEMORY LIKE MOONLIGHT

after *The persistence of Memory* By: Dali

The clock was bent
like our memory

Only focused
on what
we want
to see
and remember

it does not care
it does not dare

it can recall

what we see

it is bent
all around
all around
our vision

The clock is bent
like our memory

It does only
as told
nothing else

It senses
It feels it is
its own self

no one else's
but yet
it does
obey

Memory is
Dobby from
Harry Potter

James Apple

ALICE IN WONDERLAND

Hoping that the movie
would keep
little Goldielocks calm
until her parents
showed up
relieving me
of my duty.
I sat there
my eyes wide open
being hypnotized
by flashy colors
and anonymous characters.
I was trying to find
hidden morals
and hidden values.
Supposedly this phony illusion
of a bunny
who is always late,
a cat that disappears,
and a girl
who is trying to find the bunny
is to teach
little Goldielocks a lesson.
My eyes race
from comer to comer
as the fat, green
caterpillar
smokes out letters of the alphabet.
He makes smoking look so cool.
The rounded evil queen
with her dull, dark hair
and white roses
makes me afraid
of thick, rich people
especially ones who like white roses.
Goldielocks shows delight

with this sick illusion
of the queen beating her cards with a flamingo.
I hope she doesn't do drugs
in the future.
I hope she will never
beat anyone with a flamingo,
but seeing
how she handles her cards
during a game of speed,
my hopes are now lost.
Especially when the word "speed"
comes with excitement and a sweet smile.

Courtney Davis

Eye-Poem by Stephanie Arcamuzi

EAT YOUR VEGGIES MR. SNAKE

Katie Dillard

The morning sun reached through my window and tickled my eyelids interrupting my dancing with tigers. Today was zoo day and I was thrilled, a little too thrilled.

"Mom! Mom! Wake up! I WanDa go see the zebras!" I squealed. "They're my favorite!"

"Five more minutes Katie, please. Go read a book or something. We'll go to the zoo after lunch, I promise."

Lunchtime came as slowly as Christmas, and at tearing-off-wrapping-paper speed, I wolfed down my peanut butter and jelly sandwich and finished in time to scowl at my brother Tommy as he requested a hot dog. I sighed, doing my best to try to make him feel guilty.

"Yummy pigs," he smiled back at me as he zealously bit off a huge chunk of the offending piece of meat.

I'd been a vegetarian for as long as I could remember. Rumor had it I wouldn't even eat my meat as a baby. I just loved animals, and the thought of killing them broke my heart. So naturally I loved the zoo; seeing all those beautiful creatures always lifted my spirits and I loved getting to see them up close and personal. I couldn't wait to get there.

"Are ya'll finished yet?" I whined impatiently.

"Yeah, yeah," Mom replied stuffing the rest of her sandwich in her mouth, "you and Tommy go ahead and get in the car while I put these plates in the dishwasher."

An hour later we entered the paradise of manure and overpriced cotton candy as we headed off to admire the lions and tigers. By the time we made it through the home of the big cats, the July heat was sapping our strength and sweat ran freely down our faces.

"Hey Mom," Tommy shouted, "can we go to the reptile house now?"

"Sounds great to me; they've got air conditioning in there!"

The cool dank air assaulted us as we stepped onto the tiled floor and let our pupils adjust to the dim light. Our eyes immediately snapped to one of our favorite exhibits, the crocodiles. We always made sure to pay them a special visit, but never once had we ever seen them move, and our family constantly debated as to whether or not they were actually real. The reptiles in their tiny cages didn't fascinate me as much as the creatures housed outside, and I soon grew bored with the tiny lizard that seemed to enthrall my brother so much. As Mom read off the information card I strayed away, not far, just to the next case, but what I saw turned my short, little sheltered life topsey-turvey.

"Oh Katie, NO!" Mom yelled after me, but it was too late.

My bottom lip began to tremble and the tears spilled down my cheeks as I stood transfixed by the grotesque sight of a giant python wrapping its lean body around the lifeless body of a small gray bunny. Its once proud and perfect cotton tail alone stuck up from beneath the monster's coils like a tomato buried three-fourths of the way in spaghetti.

"COOL!" Tommy exclaimed as he loped over to see my discovery, and I promptly punched him for his impertinence.

I was so distraught that we ended up leaving shortly after "the incident" and the ride home was silent as I pondered this newly discovered cruelty of the world. My six- year-old heart was shattered, but if anyone thought that I was just going to sit back and let this happen, they had another think coming. Playing in my room later that afternoon, I had an epiphany, and for the first time in my life I had a goal—a plan for my future.

"I know what I'm going to do when I grow up!" I announced that night at dinner as I took a bite of my apple.

"What?" Mom asked, curious about my rapid emotional transformation.

I looked around and smiled proudly before proclaiming, "I'm going to make all the snakes in the reptile house vegetarians!"

Naturally I was accustomed to my parents encouraging and supporting me in everything I did, so that night their laughter rang harshly in my ears, and I didn't understand why it was so funny.

"You idiot!" Tommy chortled. "You can't make a snake become a vegetarian; it's impossible!"

I frantically searched their faces and, humiliated, I fled from the table, washing my face in tears, cursing my family, and seriously contemplating running away to live with other vegetarians who would appreciate me, although I'm sure even PETA would have laughed at my notions that day.

I described the horrors I'd seen to my friends, and while I received their mutual disgust, none of them thought I could convert snakes to vegetarians either. I refused to give up, however, writing "Save the Bunnies" and other slogans over all of my folders and hanging posters around my house.

Snakes were evil; I'd always known that, and the way I figured it, if there were no snakes I wouldn't have to go to school because we would still be in the Garden of Eden.

But still, everyone deserves a second chance, and I was determined to "make snakes nicer." Naturally, my kindergarten plan didn't go much further than that, but for the first time, I had a goal for my life, I knew what I wanted to do. Now I look back and envy that girl, so sure of her future, setting out on her own to make a difference in the world.

Eye-Poem by Mila Brinkley

THE HAIR DYE CASTROPHE

Michael Milam

Back when I was in sixth and seventh grade I dyed my hair a lot. I never used the cheap spray or pommades -- only the real deal. For a long time I had orange hair and I had grown tired of it. I wanted it to be blood red.

To achieve this effect I had to first bleach my hair. People often complain about and/or discourage using bleach because it is, in fact, every bit as harmful to hair as people say it is. After a two-hour bleaching my hair was entirely blanched, and its new consistency was comparable to straw.

Had I any common sense I would have stopped here. One is supposed to allow bleached hair at least a week or two to heal; I knew this but was willing to risk baldness. I immediately attempted to dye my hair red. After washing it out I was perturbed to discover that my hair was dark pink this agitated me enough that I made yet another foolish mistake: more hair dye.

Since the prior application did not turn out as expected, I decided to use a natural, dark red hair dye that I found under my sink. After applying this henna dye my scalp began to sear and sting beyond my pain threshold. After about thirty seconds I passed out from the excruciating hellfire on top of my head and the next thing I knew my mom had hoisted me into a sink to wash it off. Still in agony, I trudged to the shower feeling defeated, hoping for positive results.

After proper cleansing I stepped out of the shower, cleared the foggy mirror and stared in shock at my sickening head: my hair was neon pink. I returned downstairs in a stupor as my mother ran to me, excited to see my final hair color for the night.

She burst into a fit of laughter and I proclaimed dully, “I’m not going to school tomorrow. Period.” To my dismay she did not allow this blunt proposal.

That night I could barely stand to sleep on a pillow due to my scalp feeling like I had melted several layers of skin (and I may have). The next day I woke up and prepared for a day full of embarrassment. I dreaded the certain mocking and shivered at the thought of being the laughingstock of the school. However, much to my surprise, I was not the subject of mockery nor did anyone gawk or giggle at my new hairdo—quite the contrary. Everyone praised my delicious-looking cotton candy pink hair and many applauded my “bravery.”

With my ego unscathed, I returned home and greeted my mother, who was waiting at the door with still more hair dye. Unconcerned that I had already risked losing my hair once, she wanted to try another natural red color that wouldn't be quite so harsh on my scalp as the previous. I secretly was rather fond of my new pink straw, but she was less amused and (I presume) did not want to be seen in public with a pink-haired son. I allowed her to use the new dye and as I washed it out, I uneagerly checked the results in the mirror.

At that moment I wanted to hurt someone/something. After an entire previous day of excruciating pain I had returned to my starting point. This dye transformed me to the same hideous hue of orange that I had previously grown tired of. After the fiasco I put myself through, my head and hair were too fried to do anything about it for at least a month. I hate hair dye.

MY PERFECT PURPLE WORLD

C. J. Lewis

There is a vast array of colors which graces the world we live m, and I love to see this cornucopia of colors that arrange themselves before me daily. Amongst these colors, none stands in higher regard than purple. Yes, that simple color so often associated with gods and goddesses, and the historic Roman Empire. This is the very color I chose to be my symbol. Little did I know at the time, it was to become surgically attached to my spine by my own endeavors.

I suppose my love for this majestic color stems in part from my mother's own love for the color purple. From her own childhood she fell in love with the color purple, and now it appears she has passed this love of purple to the next generation. One of the benefits of a being a color enthusiast is the immense pleasure I have learned to derive from the simplest contact with a purple substance. When I see a splash of purple spring across my vision I can not help but smile. Such an apparition may become manifest in the form of a passing trick, a girl's scrunchie, or even the backpack of a fellow student. Any form of purple no matter how great, or small, grants me a momentary reprieve from the madness around me. Few can conceive the joy one can receive from the simple sighting of a purple jacket, or even a purple hat.

However, with this love for purple comes a price. I have found myself swimming in a pool of apathetic people in the realm of colors. For the average high school student red has little difference when compared to purple, or even green, but in my own case colors take on a very large role in the education process. I lose the ability to easily relate to my friends. While they thirst after "hot chicks" or the latest football score I find myself commenting on "just a shirt" or a roof that has a purple hue. In this world I thus resign myself to a search for purple belts that seem non-existent and purple animals, which appear to be exiled to realms exotic; in return I find myself left out in the cold with nothing but a purple parka for comfort.

GRANDMOTHER EARTH 2007 NATIONAL AWARDS

Poetry Award: Judge, Nancy Breen

1st	Continuing View, Carol Carpenter, Livonia, MI
2nd	Farmer's Market, Marcia Camp, Little Rock, AR
3rd	The Fifty Things Wrong With This Picture, Timothy Russell, Toronto, OH
4th	It Was Morning, Lene' Gary, Montpelier, VT
1HM	For My Parents, Anna DeMay, Orange Park, FL
2HM	To the Garden Alone, Carol Clark Williams, York, PA

Prose Awards: Judge, Frank Reed Nichols

1st	Hope Ann's Christmas, Elsie Schmied Knoke, Oak Ridge, TN
2nd	The Masher, Malu Graham, Memphis, TN
3rd	Event of the Day, Lois Requist, Benica CA
1HM	Christmas SNF, Elsie Schmied Knoke, Oak Ridge, TN

2HM Afternoon on Mt. Winton, Naomi Caldwell, Lynchburg, VA

3HM Sugar Street Hero, Mary Chase, Oklahoma City, OK

Merit:

Ardell's Ghost, Sarah Hull Gurley, Germantown, TN

How Mama Got Her Name in Lights, Judy Lee Green, Murfreesboro, TN

Homestead, Marcia Camp, Little Rock, AR

Best haiku or short form: Judge, Pat Laster

1st Drought, Donna Kennedy, Riverside, CA

2 Mockingbirds flee charred, Russell H. Strauss, Memphis, TN

3rd lightning bug, Brett Taylor, Knoxville, TN

1HM timid fledgling clings, Gloria R. Milbrath, Fort Dodge, IA

2HM Clematis climbs up, La Vonne Schoneman, Seattle, WA

3HM sun travels on long, Von S. Bourland, Happy, TX

4HM At a Loss, Angela Denise Logsdon, Memphis, TN

Humorous: Judge, Martha McNatt

1st Phone Call from Miss Muffett…Russell Strauss, Memphis, TN

2nd A Hex on my Green Thumbed Rival, Glenna Holloway, Naperville, IL

3rd A Tomcat named Aunt Bea, Jerre' Carter, Springdale, AR

1 HM My Zipper's Stuck, Russell Strauss, Memphis, TN

2 HM Cleaner Plumbing, Gloria Milbrath, Fort Dodge, IA

3HM Nobody likes a Snitch, Denna Gorrell, OK

4HM Posey, Lois Batchelor Howard, Desert
Hot Springs, CA
5HM A Doctor, Rose Camille Parrish, Jackson, TN

Environmental Awards: Judge, Marcelle Nia

1st Farewell to Summer, Anne-Marie Legan,
Herrin, IL
2nd Indian Paintbrushes, Ron Wallace, Durant,
OK
3rd Birth of a Pond, Angela Denise Logsdon,
Memphis, TN
Honorable Mentions:
The Whale's Tale, Kristin Morrill, Mendon, MA
Moon River, Anne-Marie Legan, Herrin, IL
Remnants of Past Generations, Jane E. Allen,
Wetumpka, AL
Lines, Michael Denington, Bartlett, TN
Ghostly Beauty, Winifred Hamrick Farrar,
Meridian, MS
shy cypress maidens, Sarah Hull Gurley,
Germantown, TN
Flower Bedding, Pat Crocker, Memphis, TN
Like Grass Pushing Through, Jennifer A. Jenson,
Covington, TN

2007 Grandmother Earth Student Winners
Judges, Colonial Park Writing Group

1st Daniel O'Neil, A. J. Tirrell, Germantown
High School, Billy Pullen
2nd HAIKU, Lucy Hoard, White Station
Elementary, Sarah Hamer
Alice in Wonderland, Courtney Davis,
Germantown High School, Billy Pullen

3rd Eat your Veggies, Mr. Snake, Katie Dillard, Germantown High School, Billy Pullen

You Have To, Luke Cottam Germantown High School, Billy Pullen

4th Memory Like Moonlight, James Apple, Snowden Middle School, Heather Dobbins-Combs

Catching Butterflies, Courtney Watts, Howard High School, Ellicott City, MD, Mrs. Lawrence

The Train Stops, James Apple, Snowden Middle School, Heather Dobbins-Combs

Music, the Universal Language, Ryan Johnson, White Station High School, Ms. Monique Fisher

Alone on an Unstable Wasteland, Alexis Donaldson, White Station Elementary, Sarah Hamer

The Hair Dye Castastrophe, Michael Milam, Germantown High School, Billy Pullen

Honorable Mentions:

Family, Stephanie Arcamuzi, White Station Middle School, Helen Erskine

Moonlight Dance, Katie Dillard, Germantown High School, Billy Pullen

Masterpiece Masquerade, Meredith Kahn, Germantown High School, Billy Pullen

Dancer's Canvas, Marshall Mulherin, Snowden Middle School, Heather Dobbins-Combs

Place of Perfection, Anh Vo, White Station High School, Kittie Stauffer

Johnny's Little Experiment, A Teacher's Reflection and My Perfect Purple World, all by C. J. Lewis, Germantown, High School, Billy Pullen

Memphis Bridge by Angela Logsdon

MEET THE JUDGES

Nancy Breen has two chapbooks in print: *Rites and Observances* (Finishing Line Press) and *How Time Got Away* (Pudding House Publications). She has judged poetry for *Writer's Digest*, Pennwriters, and the National Federation of State Poetry Societies. She edits *Poet's Market* and blogs at Poetic Asides (www.writersdigest.com/poeticasides).

Patricia A. Laster, Benton, Arkansas, writes a weekly general-interest column for the Amity (AR) Standard; she is a contributing editor for *Calliope: A Writer's Workshop by Mail*, based in Tucson, AZ, past president of Poets' Roundtable of Arkansas. She has spoken to or led a variety of workshops including Life Press Christian Writers's Conference. Laster has won numerous contests and has published in *Haiku Headlines, Electronic Poetry Network* (Shreveport Library), *Laurels, Parrtassus Literary Journal, Lucidity)* 37 *Cents* (e-zine) and a *Calliop*e reprint picked up by New Zealand *Freelance Writer.*

Comments on best of short poems: The majority of haiku either stretched for the 5-7-5 syllable count, used personification, were redundant, showed no images or too many. The winners' poems contained the spirit of the forms they were written in

Martha McNatt, Jackson, TN is a retired teacher and food service director. A graduate of University of Tennessee, Knoxville. She has two children and four young adult grandchildren. She has published poems and stories for more than 50 years, including, *Grandmother's Face In The Mirror;* a collection of Grandmother Stories; and *Feeding The Flock,* a Cookbook for Church Kitchens. She has been a contributor to all but one of Grandmother Earth Series.

Judging the Humor was really fun. The entries showed a wide variety of format and style and presented vivid word pictures of humorous situations. I learned from the experience and next year your entries may include some Martha humor.

Frank Reed Nichols, Memphis, TN, is author of four published books, member of the Poetry Society of Tennessee and Honorary Penguin of the NLAPW, Chickasaw Branch. Currently, he's writing short stories and a biography of Harriet Quimby, a famous flyer.

The prose entries were all hard to put down. The first part caught my interest and the middle expounded on the issues, the final paragraphs brought it all together for an ending, happy or sad. The styles that were different yet effective placed certain entries above others.

MEET THE STAFF

Mary Frances Broome lives in Germantown, TN. She is a volunteer in the office of Covenant United Methodist Church in Cordova, TN where she and her husband Bill are active members. Mary Frances was employed with Shulton, Inc./American Cyanamid Company for 30 years, and was Plant Administrative Assistant at her retirement in 1993. She received the Certified Professional Secretary rating from the National Secretaries Association in 1979. Her favorite hobby is playing Bridge, especially Duplicate Bridge.
Frances Brinkley Cowden, founder of Grandmother Earth and Life Press, received the Purple Iris Award in 2000 for outstanding contribution to the community through publishing. The Iris Awards are co-sponsored by the Memphis Branch of the National Organization of Business Women. In 2001 she was selected as one of the 50 Women Who Make a Difference by *Memphis Woman Magazine*. She is vice president of the Chickasaw Branch of NLAPW and a former president of PST.
Marcelle Zarshenas Nia, a Memphis attorney, has helped with the editing and judging of Grandmother Earth publications since its beginning in 1993. She judged the environmental and was the final judge of the student contest.

A special thanks to the Colonial Park Writing Group: **Florence Bruce, Malu Graham, Lucy Ray, Louise**

Hays and **Cindy Bebee,** for help in critiquing, pre-judging the student contest and mailing out copies of *Grandmother Earth*:

CONTRIBUTORS

Faye Adams (aloeO95@esagelink.com), De Soto, MO, has published four books of poetry, a children's book and one book of poetry and nonfiction and work in *IDEALS* and *The Ozarks Mountain*, etc. Awards include a 2006 fiction award. She is a member of Writers' Society of Jefferson County, the Missouri State Poetry Society, the Society of Children's Book Writers and Illustrators, the St. Louis Writers Guild and the Missouri Writers Guild. She is co-editing an anthology by the De Soto chapter of MSPS, and her own *Laughing with the Moon.* She has published *Pathways,*(children's poetry) and also *Chester, the Lonely Crow* and *Cookies and Blackberry Wine* and helps conduct local writer's workshops.

Jane E. Allen, Wetumpka, AL, enjoys writing fiction, nonfiction, and poetry. While she and her husband ride around the countryside in Alabama, Jane is ever watchful for new subjects for poetry and photographs. She has also been more interested in writing children's stories since the addition of six grandchildren. Jane's poem was recently published in *Whatever Remembers Us:* An *Anthology of Alabama Poetry*, and a non-fictional story will be published in *Rosie Romances and Other Stories* in the future. She is presently a member of Huntsville (AL) Branch, NLAPW, Alabama Writers' Conclave; and Women in the Arts.

Laurie Boulton, Melbourne, FL, [pen name Lauri Silver] BA, M.Ed.; retired. Published in journals and specialized magazines, *Kicker, Grapevine*, and the newspaper, *Florida Today*. Won several non-fiction short story/essay awards and numerous poetry awards in many states. Her specialty area is photography to illustrate poems for and about veterans. Two photo illustrated books, for and about veterans (free to veterans) *Echoes of the Heart* for family and friends.

Florence Bruce, Memphis, TN, is a retired medical transcriptionist. She writes and edits for local physicians. Most of her writing falls into the medical (nonfiction) category, but she has published fiction and poetry. She has won numerous awards including *Grandmother Earth's* top prose and poety awards.

Marcia Camp, Little Rock, AR, Two-time winner of the Sybil Nash Abrams Award, Marcia Camp was nominated for the Pushcart Prize in 2004. Her poetry has been anthologized in *Working the Dirt* and *Cornbread Nation*: Vol .3. "The Poet From Arkansas." Reading and dance using her poetry was_performed on Martha's_Vineyard in 2005.

Bettye Kramer Cannizzo, a Mississippi Yankee from Decatur, AL, has been widely published and has won numerous awards. Her first book of poems, *The Wmd Remembers,* won the Book of Year Award for 2004 from the Alabama State Poetry Society. In the past she has served on the State Boards as Contest Chair for the National League of American Pen Women (Huntsville branch), Alabama Conclave and the Alabama State Poetry Society. Cannizzo is currently at work on her second book of poems *From the Inside Out*. She currently maintains membership in the Poetry Society of New Hampshire and the Alabama State Poetry Society.

Carol Carpenter's stories and poems have appeared in Connecticut Review, Margie, Banyan Review, Snow Monkey, America, Barnwood, Indiana Review, Quarterly West, Carolina Quarterly and various anthologies. She received the Richard Eberhart Prize for Poetry. Formerly a college writing instructor, journalist and trainer, she now writes full time in Livonia, MI.

Jerre' Carter, Springdale, AR, is a transplanted Texan who has waited till late in life to have the courage to live her dream. She is presently writing a funny mystery with two friends, and finding out how much fun life can be.

Mary M. Chase, Oklahoma City, OK has written poetry since 1978. Expressing her grief came in poetic form. She's learned from books, other poets, and The Poetry Society of Oklahoma. She's sold stories and poetry to magazines and newspapers, published *Flashbacks of God at Work*, and self-published poetry.

Anna DeMay lives and works in Orange Park, FL. She has been writing poetry on and off for twenty years. Some of her poems have appeared in literary journals such as *West Wind Review, Grandmother Earth, Plainsongs,* and *State Street Review.*

Frieda Beasley Dorris, Memphis, TN, is one of the originators of the Dorsimbra poetry form. A past president of the Poetry Society of TN, she has won numerous awards for her poetry.

Madelyn Eastlund, Beverly Hills, FL, past president of National Federation of State Poetry Societies, is a retired instructor of Creative writing seminars and Poetry Writing Seminars. She is in her 19th year as publisher-editor of *Harp Springs Poetry Journal* and *Poets' Forum* Magazine. Her fiction, essays, and poems have appeared in various journals, magazines, anthologies, and newspapers for over 50 years.

Winifred Hamrick Farrar, Meridian, MS, is Poet Laureate of Mississippi and her work has been widely published. She is a member of the Mississippi Poetry Society, the Poetry Society of Tennessee, and the NLAPW, Chickasaw Branch.

Lene' Gary, Montpelier, VT, has won numerous awards for both poetry and prose. Her recent publications include *SAGE, Watershed, Vermont Nature, KNOCK; NEWN; and The Poet's Touchstone.* When she's not writing, she can be found paddling her well-worn Mad River canoe.

Dena R. Gorrell, Edmond, OK, and has been writing poetry since age nine. She wins 75 to 100 awards per year and was named Poet Laureate of the Poetry Society of Oklahoma for 2004 and 2005. She has published four books of poetry.

Malu Graham, Memphis, TN, won the Hackney Award for fiction (Birmingham Southern College). She has poems and short stories published in *St. Petersburg Times, Emerald Coast Review, Octoberfest Magazine,* and *Broomstick.* She has won prizes in fiction from Florida Writers' Competition and from Life Press. She is the present Poet Laureate of PST.

Sarah Hull Gurley is a member of PST. She was born and reared in Louisiana. She has a degree in Business Administration from Louisiana Technical College and is a member of St. Luke's United Methodist Church. She is currently residing in Germantown, TN and Leesburg, FL.

Sandra Hancock lives on the Big Sandy River in Benton Co, TN. She is a second grade teacher at Camden Elementary School and belongs to three writers' groups.

Louise Hays, Collierville, TN, is an active member of the Poetry Society of TN.

Verna Lee Hinegardner, Hot Springs, AR, was Poet Laureate of Arkansas for 13 years. She is past president of the AR Pioneer Branch of NLAPW; Past President of PRA; President of Roundtable Poets of Hot Springs; served 12 years on the board of NFSPS and chaired two of their national conventions; member of Poets' Study Club, Poetry Society of America, International Poetry Society, and is listed in The International Directory of Distinguished Leadership. Hinegardner was inducted into the AR Writers' Hall of

Fame in 1991; won their Sybil Nash Abrams Award in 1973, 1979 and 1991; and received the AR Award of Merit in 1976 and 1983; and is the author of twelve books of poetry.

Glenna Holloway, Naperville, IL, is published in *North American Review, Michigan Quarterly Review, Notre Dame Review,* and many others including THE PUSHCART PRIZE, 2001, awarded by Illinois Arts Council Fellowship, 2005. She is founding president of the Illinois State Poetry Society, 1991 and is currently working on her first poetry book.

Elizabeth Howard, Crossville, TN, is the author of *Gleaners*, Grandmother Earth 2005 and *Anemones,* Grandmother Earth, 1998. A frequent award-winner, she writes both poetry and fiction. Her work has been published in *Big Muddy, Appalachian Journal, Wind, Poem, Cold Mountain Review, Comstock Review,* and other journals.

Lois Batchelor Howard, Desert Hot Springs, CA, a multi-award winning published writer, is a graduate of The University of Michigan in Music. She loves the music of words as well as the sounds of music itself!

Jennifer A. Jenson lives with her husband Richard D. Cartwright and their seven cats in Covington, TN, where they have recently relocated from Memphis. Retired from a career in the legal field, she spends her days writing poetry and enjoying small town life.

Faye Williams Jones, North Little Rock, AR, is a retired school librarian who received numerous awards during her career. She presented workshops at state, regional, national, and international library and media conferences. Memberships include PRA and River Market Poets Branch. She and her husband, Bob Jones, collaborate to create framed poetry and photography exhibits.

Donna Kennedy, Riverside, CA, has appeared in *Ternenos* magazine and *Poetic Medicine: The Healing Art of Poem-Making* by John Fox. She was a feature writer for a large California newspaper for years and now writes fiction and teaches English at a local college.

Elsie Schmied Knoke, Oak Ridge, TN, says she has always written. During her nursing career she published two textbooks for nurse managers and articles in professional journals. Now she writes fiction and nonfiction for pleasure. She has four children, five granddaughters and one great-granddaughter. She travels extensively with her second husband.

Susan Leeds, Delray Beach, FL, has won 1st Prize (Haiku) in *Grandmother Earth IX*, Finalist, Robert Penn Warren Awards, 3rd Prize, Vi Bagliore Memorial Award (NLAPW), etc. Publications include: *Midwest Poetry Review, Pegasus, Pen Women Magazine, Lucidit,,Sun-Sentinel* newspaper (on-line), etc. Member—NLAPW, FLSA.

Anne-Marie Legan, Herrin, IL, received from Cader Publishing, Ltd., the 1998 International Poet Of The Year Chapbook Competition, $5000 grand prize and publication of *My Soul's On A Journey.* Active in Southern IL Writer's Guild, she has received many awards and been published widely, including twelve poetry books (four published in Italy) and four mystery novels, *Tattoo of a Wolf Spider, Deadly Chase, Death Shadow* and her latest mystery novel *Wolf Lake.*

Angela Logsdon, Memphis, TN,is a descendant of the Cherokee/Choctaw nations. She strives to reflect the beauty of her heritage in her writing. Her poetry and photography has been previously published in *Grandmother Earth*. She is a member of PST.

Gloria R. Milbrath, Fort Dodge, IA, is a mother of five, grandmother of nine and is enjoying remission from stage 4 lymphoma, thanks in part to an autologous adult stem cell transplant. She's had poems published locally, in *Grandmother Earth, Lucidity, The Lutheran Message, Lyrical Iowa* and others. Her husband of 47 years provides untiring support.

Rose Camille Parish, Jackson, TN, graduated from Merry High School and Lane College and then moved to Memphis until she retired in 1994 to Jackson.

Lucile Roberts Ray, Memphis, TN is author of a collection of poetry and prose, *Gifts: Extraordinaries from an Ordinary Life.*

Lois Requist, Benicia, CA, likes to travel, bicycle, hike, read, go to the theatre, and enjoy her family and the camaraderie of eating with friends. While she never made a living at writing, she has made a life. Writing helps her deal with the difficulties in life and celebrate the pleasures.

Timothy Russell, Toronto, OH, publishes work here and there, now and then. He lives at mile 61 on the Ohio River.

LaVonne Schoneman, Seattle, WA, is a former actress. Her husband, children and eight grandchildren also reside in WA. She is author of the popular "How to Cope" series on coping with post-polio. She also writes (and judges) fiction and poetry.

N. Colwell Snell, Salt Lake City, UT, is a native of Wyoming. His poetry has won awards locally and nationally and has been published in several anthologies, including *Byline*, *Poetry Panorama, Encore, Bay Area Poets Coalition, California Quarterly, Grandmother Earth* and *Anthology Literary Magazine.* Co-author of *By the Throat, Selected Poems*, he has been featured "In the Spotlight" of *Poet's Forum Magazine.* He is the current president of the Utah State Poetry Society and the editor of *Utah Sings, Volume VIII.*

Madalyn McKnight Stanford, Memphis, TN, is the wife of a pediatrician, a mother, a grandmother, and an actress in local community theatres. She loves the outdoors and travel. She ia a retired Wildlife

Rehabilitation Coordinator and Technician, State Wildlife Resources agency.

Russell H. Strauss, Memphis, TN, has served twice as president of the Poetry Society of Tennessee and is currently serving as second vice-president of the National Federation of State Poetry Societies. He has been published in every issue of Grandmother Earth beginning with *Grandmother Earth II.*

Brett Taylor, Knoxville, TN, is originally from Wartburg, TN. In addition to *Grandmother Earth*, he has been published in *Soul Fountain, The Nocturnal Lyric, South by SouthEast, Raw Nervz Haiku, Haiku Headlines, Persimmon, Modern Haiku, Cicada, ampersand, Nisqually, Delta Review, Haiku Novine, Red Owl, splizz* and *Cotyledon*.

Vincent J. Tomeo, Flushing, NY, has published 507 poems in publications such as *The New York Times, Comstock Review, Mid-America Poetry Review* and *Grandmother Earth* (VII through XI).

Ron Wallace, Durant, OK, is of Choctaw, Cherokee, Osage and Scots-Irish heritage. His first book *Native Son* was a finalist in the 2007 Oklahoma Book Awards. He is a member of the Poetry Society of Oklahoma and emergingpoets.net writing groups. His work also appears in a number of magazines, literary magazines and anthologies.

Carol Clark Williams, York, PA, is a retail sales manager who would rather write poetry. She is a rostered poet with the Pennsylvania Arts in Education program, and teaches poetry workshops to high schools students, senior citizens, support groups, and residents of institutions.

STUDENT CONTRIBUTORS

James Apple, Memphis, TN, was a 7th grade student of Mrs. Heather Dobbins-Combs at Snowden School when he wrote his poems.

Stephanie Arcamuzi, Memphis, TN, was in the 8th Grade at White Station Middle School, Her teacher was Mrs. Helen Erskine.

Mila Brinkley is in the fourth grade at Bailey Station Elementary in Collierville, TN. She is the daughter of Clay and Marena Brinkley. She loves art and writing.

Luke Cottam, Grade 11 **, Courtney Davis,** Grade 10, **Katie Dillard,** Grade 12, **C. J. Lewis,** Grade 11, **Michael Milam,** Grade 12, **and A. J. Tirrell,** Grade 11 were all students of Bill Pullen of Germantown High School in Germantown, TN. Mr. Pullen's students are repeatedly winners in local and national contests.

Lucy Hoard, Memphis, TN was a student in Mrs. Sarah Hamer's third grade class when she wrote her poem.

Ryan Johnson, Memphis, TN, was in the 11th grade at White Station High School with Ms. Monique Fisher as his teacher when he made his Eye-Poem.

Courtney Watts, Ellicott City, MD, has been a student winner for five years. He was in the 10th Grade at Howard High School when he wrote his poem

GRANDMOTHER EARTH PUBLICATIONS

Prices quoted here include media postage and apply only if ordered directly from Grandmother Earth.

***Gleaners* by Elizabeth Howard**

cover and art by Jennifer Quillen.

This second collection contains **award winning and previously published poetry** about life in rural East Tennessee. Grandmother Earth previously published *Anemones* by Howard. ISBN 1-884289-47-9.$10

***Crystal and Creatures* by Clovita Rice**

Photographs by Gary Fountain.

This collection of favorite poetry from the former editor of the literary magazine, *Voices International*, contains many selections which **previously appeared** in a variety of publications over four decades. ISBN: 1-884289-49-5. $10

Abbott, Barbara, *GRANDMOTHER EARTH'S HEALTHY AND WISE COOKBOOK*, 1-884289-13-4. Healthy and easy cooking, but not diet. First layer of fat skimmed from Southern cooking. Optabind binding; List $11.95— $9.

Benedict, Burnette Bolin, *KINSHIP*, 1-884289-08. Lyrical poetry by Knoxville poet. Chapbook, 1995, $6.

Cowden, Frances Brinkley *BUTTERFLIES AND UNICORNS*, ED 4, 1-884289-04-5 (Cowden and Hatchett) Poetry for the young and young-at-heart with notes on teaching creative writing. PB, 1994, List 8.95—$6.

TO LOVE A WHALE; 1-884289-06-1. Learn about endangered animals from children and educators. Children's drawings, poetry and prose, PB (Perfect bound) 1995, List $14.95—$6.

Cowden, Frances Brinkley, *VIEW FROM A MISSISSIPPI RIVER COTTON SACK*, 1-884289-03-7. Illustrated by the author. This collection of prize-winning poetry and short prose emphasizes farm life in Mississippi County, Arkansas.

Cloth, gold imprint, with dust jacket 1993, List $21.95—Sale $10, while supply lasts.

Daniel, Jack, *SOUTHERN RAILWAY- FROM STEVENSON TO MEMPHIS*—1-884289-17-7. 8 1/2x 11with 400+ photographs, 360 pages, 1996. Daniel is an Alabama native who now lives in Cordova, TN. Documents and other papers with emphasis upon history of Southern Railway and its workers. PB, $75. Out of Print. **Limited supply.**

MY RECOLLECTIONS OF CHEROKEE, ALABAMA, 1-884289-25, 8 1/2x11. 300+ photographs of author's family history and life in early Cherokee, 232 pages, PB, 1998, $25.

THOROUGHBREDS OF RAILROADING: YESTERDAY AND TODAY, ISBN 1-884289-26-6 1999, 312 pages, 8 1/2x 11, pictorial history of several railroads. Similar to his other railroad book PB, $30.

Hatchett, Eve Braden, *TAKE TIME TO LAUGH*: It's the Music of the Soul. 1- 884289-00-2. Humorous poetry taking off on Eden theme. Chapbook, **very limited edition**, 1993, $9.

Howard, Elizabeth, *ANEMONES*, 1-884289-27-4, Prize-winning poetry, all previously published, East Tennessee (Crossville) poet, introduction by Connie Green, creative writing instructor, U.T. 1998, $9.

GLEANERS, 1-884289-47-9. More excellent previously published and prize-winning poems, 2005, $10

Rice, Clovita, *CRYSTAL and CREATURES,* 1-884289-49-5 A collection of prize-winning and previously published poetry by the editor of Voices International. In 1998 she was inducted into the Arkansas Hall of fame. 2005, $10.

Schirz, Shirley Rounds, *ASHES TO OAK*, 1-884289-07-X Poetry of the lakes region by widely-published Wisconsin author. Grandmother Earth chapbook winner, 1995, $6.

***GRANDMOTHER EARTH* SERIES:** $7 each (multiple copies $6 each, Volumes II and III are $4) Order by Volume number.

GRANDMOTHER EARTH II, III and X feature Tennessee writers. Volume IV features Arkansas Writers. Volume VII features Alabama writers. Volume VIII features Mississippi. Volume IX features Florida writers. Volume 13 features Oklahoma.

LIFE PRESS PUBLICATIONS

Boren, Blanche S., *THORNS TO VELVET. Devotionals from a Lifetime of Christian Experience.* 1-884289-231, Blanche S. Boren, Kivar 7, gold imprint, cloth, List 19.95—$12.

Cowden, Frances Brinkley, *OUR GOLDEN THREAD: Dealing with Grief,* 1-884289-10-x, Ed. Personal testimonies and poetry of 40 contributors from clergy and lay writers who deal with different kinds of grief using personal experiences in their faith journeys. Kivar 7 cloth, gold imprint, 1996,

List $18— $12.

ANGELS MESSENGERS OF LOVE AND GRACE, 1-884289-18-5. True stories of angel experiences by contributors from all walks of life. 96 pages, perfect bound, 1999, $10.

TOWARD IMAGERY AND FORM: A WRITER'S NOTE-BOOK, 1-8884289-29-0. Loose leaf or coil notebook which contains lessons on strengthening writing skills though poetry and prose lessons. Editing, imagery and poetry forms are stressed. Many forms used are explained. Prize-winning examples by contemporary poets. Lessons were from the first five years of Life Press Writers' Association. $8.

Crow, Geraldine Ketchum, BLOOM WHERE YOU ARE TRANSPLANTED, 1-884289-12-6. A resident of Little Rock, Arkansas, Crow grew up in Hot Springs and tells of life in Perry County where she and her husband farmed for several years. Humorous, inspirational approach about moving from the city to the country. 1996, List 11.95—$8.

Davis, Elaine Nunnally, *MOTHERS OF JESUS: FROM MATTHEW'S GENEALOGY,* 1-884289-05-3. Biography of five women mentioned in Matthew. 344 pp. PB, 1994, List $15.95—$10.

EVES FRUIT, 1-884289-11-8, Defense of Eve and implications for the modern woman. PB, 1995,

List #15.95—$8 .

MEMORIALS

Donna Sue Tacker

November 16, 1942—June 21, 2007

Wife of Robert A. Tacker;
Mother of Judy and Ben Meyer, Missy and Ricky Cato, Nikki and Jim Speer, Juliane and Brandon Veach, Joe and Katy Tacker, Bret and Barbara Tacker, Chris and Jaylene Tacker, 24 grandchildren and five great-grandchildren.

Robert Lee Simonton

September 19, 1925—June 11, 2007

Honorary Member and Former President Of the Poetry Society of Tennessee

Judy D. Duck

December 8,1945—September 9, 2007
Wife of Harvey Duck
Sister of Jane Stanley Terry,
Lindsay and Wallace Chandler

PATRONS

INDEX

STUDENTS